A LARGE PRINT

PRAYER BOOK

All booklets are published
thanks to the generous support
of the members of the
Catholic Truth Society

CATHOLIC TRUTH SOCIETY
PUBLISHERS TO THE HOLY SEE

Contents

Morning Prayers

The Sign of the Cross

In the name of the Father and of the Son and of the Holy Spirit Amen.

I thank you, Lord, for the wonder of my being, for giving me another day to love and serve you. May I often think of you during today!
Dear Lord, inspire everything

we say and do this day. May it all begin from you and with your unfailing help be carried through for your glory. We ask this through Christ our Lord.

Strengthen in your love and in their vocation our Holy Father, the Pope, all bishops and priests and other ministers. Lord hear my prayer.

Guide the leaders of the nations to establish the rule of justice for peace for the whole human family. Lord hear my prayer.

Bless all Christian families, particularly my own loved ones. May the light of your presence shine out to the world from them. Lord hear my prayer.

NIGHT PRAYERS

My God, from my heart I thank you for the many blessings you have given to me. I thank you for having created me and for having placed me in your holy catholic church; and for having given me so many graces and mercies through the merits of Jesus Christ. And I thank you, dear Jesus, for having become a little child for my sake, to teach me to be holy and humble like you; and for having died on the cross that I might have pardon for all my sins and get to heaven. Also I thank you for all your other mercies, most of all for those you have given to me today.

Bless all who give their lives and prayer and work for the building up of your kingdom.

Send your Church many good priests and religious. Inspire young people to be generous and prompt in responding to your call. Lord hear my prayer.

Urge all Christian people to care for your Son who suffers in the hungry and the homeless, by showing them true compassion and giving effective help. Lord hear my prayer.

Enlighten all governments to uphold sound moral standards and so help to dispel the darkness of sin from your creation. Lord hear my prayer.

At the end of this day, Lord, I thank you for all your love and help.

O my God, I thank you for all the benefits which I have ever received from you and especially this day. Give me light to see what sins I have committed and grant me grace to be truly sorry for them.

[Here examine your conscience for the faults you have committed during the day.]

O my God, because you are so good, I am very sorry that I have sinned against you and by the help of your grace I will not sin again.

May our Blessed Lady, St Joseph and all the Saints pray for us to the Lord, that we may be preserved this night from sin and all evil. Amen.

O my good Angel, whom God has appointed to be my guardian, watch over me during this night. Angels and Saints of God, pray for me.

The Lord bless us and keep us from all evil and bring us to everlasting life.

May the souls of the faithful departed, through the mercy of God, rest in peace.

Into your hands, O Lord, I commend my spirit. Lord Jesus, receive my soul. In the name of Our Lord Jesus Christ, crucified, I lay me down to rest. Bless me, O Lord, and defend me; preserve me from a sudden and unprovided death and from all dangers, and bring me to life everlasting with you. Amen.

THE HOLY ROSARY

The Joyful Mysteries are said on Mondays and Saturdays, the Luminous on Thursdays, the Sorrowful on Tuesdays and Fridays and the Glorious on Wednesdays and Sundays.
The twenty mysteries are:

I. The Five Joyful Mysteries

1. The Annunciation
2. The Visitation
3. The Nativity

4. The Presentation in the Temple
5. The Finding of the Child Jesus in the Temple

II. The Five Luminous Mysteries

1. The Baptism in the Jordan
2. The Wedding at Cana
3. The Proclamation of the Kingdom of God
4. The Transfiguration
5. The Institution of the Eucharist

III. The Five Sorrowful Mysteries

1. The Prayer and Agony in the Garden
2. The Scourging at the Pillar
3. The Crowning with Thorns
4. The Carrying of the Cross
5. The Crucifixion and Death of Our Lord

IV. The Five Glorious Mysteries

1. The Resurrection
2. The Ascension of Christ into Heaven
3. The Descent of the Holy

Spirit on the Apostles
4. The Assumption
5. The Coronation of the Blessed Virgin Mary in Heaven and the Glory of all the Saints

The Apostles' Creed

I believe in God, the Father almighty, creator of heaven and earth. I believe in Jesus Christ, his only Son, our Lord. He was conceived by the power of the Holy Spirit and born of the Virgin Mary. He suffered under Pontius Pilate, was crucified, died and was buried. He descended to the dead. On the third day he rose again. He ascended into heaven and is seated at the right hand of the Father. He will come again to judge the living and the dead. I believe in the Holy Spirit, the holy Catholic church, the communion of saints, the forgiveness of sins, the resurrection of the body and life everlasting. Amen.

Our Father

Our Father who art in heaven hallowed be thy name. Thy kingdom come. Thy will be done on earth as it is in heaven. Give us this day our daily bread, and forgive us our trespasses, as we forgive those who trespass against us. And lead us not into temptation but deliver us from evil. Amen.

Hail Mary

Hail Mary, full of grace, the Lord is with thee. Blessed art thou among women and blessed is the fruit of thy womb, Jesus. Holy Mary, Mother of God, pray for us sinners, now and in the hour of our death. Amen.

Glory be

Glory be to the Father and to the Son and to the Holy Spirit as it was in the beginning is now and ever shall be world without end. Amen.

Fatima Prayer

O my Jesus forgive us our sins. Save us from the fires of hell. Lead all souls to heaven, especially those most in need of your mercy.

Prayer for the Dead

Eternal rest grant unto them, O Lord and let perpetual light shine upon them.

Hail Holy Queen

Hail, holy Queen, Mother of Mercy, hail, our life, our sweetness and our hope. To thee do we cry, poor banished children of Eve; to thee do we send up our sighs, mourning and weeping in this valley of tears. Turn then, most gracious advocate, thine eyes of mercy towards us; and after this our exile, show unto us the blessed fruit of thy womb Jesus. O clement, O loving, O sweet Virgin Mary.

V. Pray for us O holy Mother of God.
R. That we may be made worthy
of the promises of Christ.

Concluding Prayer

O God, whose only-begotten
Son, by his life, death and resurrection, has purchased for us the
rewards of eternal life; grant we
beseech thee, that meditating on
these mysteries of the most holy
rosary of the Blessed Virgin
Mary, we may both imitate what
they contain and obtain what
they promise, through the same
Christ Our Lord.

GOSPEL CANTICLES

The Benedictus

Blessed be the Lord, the God of Israel He has visited His people and redeemed them. He has raised up for us a mighty saviour in the house of David his servant, as he promised by the lips of holy men those who were his prophets from of old. A saviour who would free us from our foes from the hands of all who hate us. So his love for our fathers is fulfiled and his holy covenant remembered. He swore to Abraham our father to grant us that, free from fear and saved from the hands of our foes, we might serve him in holiness and justice all the days of our life in his presence. As for you, little child, you shall be called a prophet of God the Most High. You shall go ahead of the Lord to prepare his way before him, to make known to his people their salvation through forgiveness of all their sins, the loving-kindness

of the heart of our God who vis-
its us like the dawn from on
high. He will give light to those
in darkness those who dwell in
the shadow of death, and guide
us into the way of peace.

The Magnificat

My soul glorifies the Lord, my
spirit rejoices in God my
Saviour. He looks on his servant
in her lowliness; henceforth all
ages will call me blessed. The
Almighty works marvels for
me. Holy his name! His mercy
is from age to age, on those

who fear him. He puts forth his arm in strength and scatters the proud-hearted. He casts the mighty from their thrones and raises the lowly. He fills the starving with good things, sends the rich away empty. He protects Israel, his servant, remembering his mercy, the mercy promised to our fathers, to Abraham and his sons for ever.

The Nunc Dimittis

At last all-powerful Master, you give leave to your servant to go in peace, according to your promise. For my eyes have seen your salvation which you have prepared for all the nations, the light to enlighten the gentiles and give glory to Israel, your people.

WELL-LOVED PRAYERS

Memorare

Remember, O most loving Virgin Mary, that it is a thing unheard of that anyone ever had recourse to your protection, implored your help, or sought your intercession, and was left forsaken. Filled therefore with confidence in your goodness, I fly to you, O Mother, Virgin of virgins, To you I come, before you I stand, a sorrowful sinner. Despise not my poor words, O Mother of the Word of God, but graciously hear and grant my prayer. Amen.

Act of Faith

I accept all that you teach me, Lord, through your church, because your word is true. I believe, Lord help my unbelief!

Act of Hope

I have complete confidence in your promise calling me to eternal life. Give me all the help I need to remain true to you. Sacred Heart of Jesus I place all my trust in you!

Act of Charity

Fill my heart with the spirit of your love, so that I may love you with all my heart and share that love of yours with others. Father, hallowed be thy name!

Regina Caeli

Queen of heaven, rejoice, alleluia. For Christ your Son and Son of God has risen as he said, alleluia. Pray to God for us, alleluia. Rejoice and be glad, O Virgin Mary, alleluia For the Lord has truly risen, alleluia. God of life, you have given joy to the world by the resurrection of your Son, our Lord, Jesus Christ. Through the prayers of his mother, the Virgin Mary, bring us to the happiness of eternal life. We ask this through Christ our Lord. Amen.

Prayer to St Michael

St Michael, the Archangel, defend us in the day of battle;

be our safeguard against the wickedness and snares of the devil. May God rebuke him, we humbly pray and do you, O Prince of the heavenly host, by the power of God, cast into hell Satan and all the other evil spirits who prowl through the world seeking the ruin of souls. Amen.

In Temptation

Lord, save me or I perish. Keep me close to you by your grace or I shall sin and fall away from you. Lord, I am very weak; give me grace and make my will strong that I may not sin. Jesus, help me; Mary, help me; my holy angel watch over me.

In Trouble

In all things may the most holy, the most just, and the most lovable will of God be done, praised and exalted above all for ever. Your will be done, O Lord, your will be done. The Lord has given, the Lord has taken away. Blessed be the name of the Lord.

In Sickness and Pain

Lord, your will be done. I take this for my sins. I offer up to you my sufferings, together with all that my Saviour has suffered for me; and I beg of you, through his sufferings to have mercy on me. Free me from this illness and pain if it is your will, and if it is for my good. You love me too much to let me suffer unless it is for my good. Therefore O Lord, I trust myself to you. Do with me as you please. In sickness and health I wish to love you always.

For Purity

O Jesus, most pure of heart! O spotless Lamb of God! Help me so that I may keep my heart and body pure, that all through my life I may never displease you by any wicked thing. Give me the blessing of the clean of heart.

Acceptance of Death

O Lord my God, I now, at this moment, readily and willingly accept at your hand whatever kind of death it may please you to send me, with all its pains, penalties and sorrows.

O Sacrament Most Holy

O Sacrament Most Holy,
O Sacrament Divine, All praise
and all thanksgiving be every
moment thine.

Anima Christi

Soul of Christ, sanctify me.
Body of Christ, heal me. Blood
of Christ, drench me. Water
from the side of Christ, wash
me. Passion of Christ, strengthen
me. Good Jesus, hear me. In
your wounds shelter me. From
turning away keep me. From the
evil one protect me. At the hour

of my death call me. Into your presence lead me, to you praise with all your saints for ever and ever. Amen.

Act of Consecration

O Sacred Heart of Jesus, filled with infinite love, broken by my ingratitude, pierced by my sin, yet loving me still, accept the consecration that I make to you of all that I have and all that I am. Take every faculty of my soul and body and draw me day by day nearer to your sacred side and there as I may bear the lesson, teach me your blessed ways. Amen.

De Profundis
Psalm 130

Out of the depths I cry to you, O Lord, Lord, hear my voice! O let your ears be attentive to the voice of my pleading. If you, O Lord, should mark our guilt, Lord, who would survive? But with you is found forgiveness; for this we revere you. My soul is waiting for the Lord, I count on his word. My soul is longing for the Lord more than watchmen for daybreak. Let the watchman count on daybreak and Israel on the Lord. Because with the Lord there is mercy and fullness of redemption, Israel indeed he will redeem from all its iniquity.

Prayer to our Guardian Angel

Angel sent by God to guide me, be my light and walk beside me; be my guardian and protect me; on the paths of life direct me.

Veni Sancte Spiritus

Come, Holy Spirit, fill the hearts of your faithful And kindle in them the fire of your love. Send forth your Spirit and they shall be created And you will renew the face of the earth. Lord, by the light of your Holy Spirit you have taught the hearts of your faithful. In that same Spirit help us to relish what is right and always rejoice in your consolation. We ask this through Christ our Lord. Amen.

Prayer for the Dead

O God, the creator and redeemer of all the faithful, grant to the souls of your departed servants the remission of all their sins, that through pious supplications they may obtain that pardon which they have always desired; who lives and reigns for ever and ever. Amen.

Prayer for the Pope

O almighty and eternal God, have mercy on your servant, our Pope, and direct him according to your clemency into the way of everlasting salvation; that he may desire by your grace those things that are agreeable to you and perform them with all his strength. Through Christ our Lord. Amen.

Prayer for Priests

Father, you appointed your Son Jesus Christ eternal high priest. Guide those he has chosen to be ministers of word and sacrament and help them to be faithful in fulfiling the ministry they have received. Grant this through our

Lord Jesus Christ, your Son, who lives and reigns with you and the Holy Spirit, one God for ever and ever. Amen.

Prayer for Vocations

Lord Jesus Christ, Shepherd of souls who called the apostles to be fishers of men, raise up new apostles in your holy church. Teach them that to serve you is to reign; to possess you is to possess all things. Kindle in the young hearts of our sons and daughters the fire of zeal for souls. Make them eager to spread your kingdom on this earth. Grant them courage to follow you, who are the Way, the Truth, and the Life, who live and reign for ever and ever.

Mary, Queen of the clergy, pray for us. Help our students who are preparing for the priesthood.

Prayer for Unity

O Lord, Jesus Christ, who said to your apostles, 'Peace I leave with you, my peace I give to you.' Look not on our sins but on the faith of your church and grant her that peace and unity which is according to your will; who live and reign for ever and ever Amen.

Prayer for Peace

Give peace, O Lord in our days for there is no other to fight for us but only you our God. May peace be ours through your protection, O Lord, and prosperity through your strong defence. O God, from whom are holy desires, right counsels and just deeds, give to your servants that peace which the world cannot give; that we may serve you with our whole hearts and live quiet lives under your protection, free from the fear of our enemies. Through Christ our Lord. Amen.

PRAYERS BEFORE AND AFTER CONFESSION

Before Confession

O Lord Jesus Christ, lover of my soul, I grieve from the bottom of my heart that I have offended you, my most loving redeemer, to whom all sin is infinitely displeasing; who have so loved me that you shed your blood for me and endured the bitter torments of a most cruel death.

O my God, O infinite goodness, would that I had never offended thee.

Almighty and merciful God, you have brought me here in the name of your Son to receive your mercy and grace in my time of need. Open my eyes to see the evil I have done. Touch my heart and convert me to yourself. Where sin has separated me from you, may your love unite me to you again; where sin has brought weakness, may your power heal and strengthen; where sin has brought death, may your spirit raise to new life. Give me a new heart to love you so that my life may reflect the image of your Son. May the world see the glory of Christ revealed in your church and come to know that he is the one whom you have sent, Jesus Christ, your Son, our Lord. Amen.

I Confess

I confess to almighty God and to you, my brothers and sisters, that I have sinned through my own fault, in my thoughts and in my words, in what I have done and in what I have failed to do; and I ask blessed Mary, ever virgin, all the angels and saints and you, my brothers and sisters, to pray for me to the Lord our God. Amen.

Act of Faith

O my God, I believe in you because you are truth itself, and I believe in all that the Catholic Church believes and teaches, because you have revealed it. Give me a firmer faith and help me to act according to my faith.

Acts of Contrition

My God, I am sorry for my sins with all my heart. In choosing to do wrong and failing to do good, I have sinned against you whom I should love above all things. I firmly intend, with your help, to do penance, to sin no more, and to avoid whatever leads me to sin. Our Saviour Jesus Christ suffered and died for us. In his name, my God, have mercy. Amen.

O my God I am very sorry that I have offended you, because you are so good and I will not sin again.

I firmly resolve to forsake and flee from all sins, to avoid the occasion of them and to confess all those sins which I have committed against your divine goodness and to love you, my God for your own sake above all things forever. Grant me the grace to do so, O most gracious Lord Jesus.

My Lord and God, I sincerely acknowledge myself to be a vile and wretched sinner unworthy to appear in your presence. But have mercy on me and I will be saved.

O most merciful and forgiving Lord, for love of you, I forgive all who have ever offended me.

Prayer for Forgiveness

Lord, hear the prayers of those who confess to you and in your merciful love give us your pardon. Amen.

After Confession

O almighty and merciful God, who, according to the multitude of your tender mercies, have been pleased once more to receive me, after so many times going astray from you, and to admit me to this sacrament of forgiveness, I give you thanks with all the powers of my soul for this and all other mercies, graces and blessings bestowed upon me, and casting myself at your sacred feet, I offer myself to be henceforth forever yours. Let nothing in life or death ever separate me from you. From this moment I give myself eternally to your love and service. Grant that for the time to come I may hate sin more than death itself, and avoid all such occasions and company as have unhappily brought me to it. This I resolve to do by the aid of your divine grace, without which I can do nothing. I beg your blessing on these my resolutions. Give me grace to be now and always a true penitent; through Jesus Christ your Son. Amen.

PRAYERS FOR HOLY COMMUNION

Before Holy Communion

Prayer for Help

O my God, help me to make a good communion. Mary, my dearest mother pray to Jesus for me. My dear guardian angel, lead me to the altar of God.

Act of Faith

O God, because you have said it,

I believe that I shall receive the sacred body of Jesus Christ to eat and his precious blood to drink. My God, I believe this with all my heart.

Act of Humility

My God, I confess that I am not worthy to receive the body and blood of Jesus, on account of my sins. Lord I am not worthy that you should enter under my roof but say the word and my soul shall be healed.

Act of Sorrow

My God, I detest all the sins of

my life. I am sorry for them, because they have offended you, my God, who are so good. I resolve never to commit sin any more. My good God, pity me, have mercy on me, forgive me.

Act of Adoration

O Jesus, great God, present on the altar, I bow down before you. I adore you.

Act of Love

Sweet Jesus, I love you. I desire with all my heart to receive you. Most sweet Jesus, come into my poor soul and give me your whole self, body, blood, soul and divinity that I may live forever with you.

After Holy Communion

Act of Adoration

O Jesus, my God, my creator, I adore you, because from your hands I came and with you I am to be happy forever.

Act of Humility

O Jesus, I am but dust and ashes and yet you have come to me and my poor heart may speak to you.

Act of Love

Sweet Jesus, I love you. I love you with all my heart. You know that I love you and wish to love you daily more and more.

Act of Thanksgiving

My good Jesus, I thank you with all my heart. How good, how kind you are to me sweet Jesus! Blessed be Jesus in the most holy sacrament of the altar.

Act of Offering

O Jesus, receive my poor offering. Jesus, you have given yourself to me and now let me give myself to you: I give you my body that it may be chaste and pure. I give you my soul that it may be free from sin. I give you my heart that it may always love you. I give you every breath that I breathe, and especially my last; I give you myself in life and death, that I may be yours forever.

Prayer before a Crucifix

O kind and most sweet Jesus, I cast myself on my knees in your sight and with the most

fervent desire of my soul, I pray
and beseech you to impress on
my heart faith, hope and charity
with true repentance for my sins
and a firm desire of amendment,
while with deep affection and
grief of soul I contemplate your
five most precious wounds;
having before my eyes what
David said in prophecy of you,
O good Jesus: 'They pierced
my hands and my feet; they
have numbered all my bones.'
Sweet Jesus, you are with me
by your grace. I will never

leave you by mortal sin for though I am weak, I have such hope in you. Give me the grace to persevere. Amen.

THE DIVINE PRAISES

Blessed be God. Blessed be his holy Name. Blessed be Jesus Christ, true God and true Man. Blessed be the name of Jesus. Blessed be his most Sacred Heart. Blessed be his most Precious Blood. Blessed be Jesus in the most holy Sacrament of the Altar. Blessed be the Holy Spirit, the Paraclete. Blessed be the great Mother of God, Mary, most holy. Blessed be her holy and Immaculate Conception. Blessed be her glorious Assumption. Blessed be the name of Mary, Virgin and Mother. Blessed be St Joseph, her spouse most chaste. Blessed be God in his Angels and Saints.